AVOCADO HIGHWAY

30 Ways To Make The Most Of Your Avocado Toast

Take a ride on the avocado Highway
♡ Pam & Robi

ROBI KELLERMAN & PAMELA FINK

Berkshires | New York City

AVOCADO HIGHWAY
30 Ways To Make The Most Of Your Avocado Toast
By Robi Kellerman and Pamela Fink

Published in 2018 by
Avocado Highway
P.O. Box 268
South Egremont, MA 01258
avocadohighway@gmail.com

ISBN: 978-0-692-92039-8
Second Edition

Printed in the United States of America

Food Stylist: Frances Boswell
Photography: Beatriz da Costa
Recipe Editor: Susan Simon
Design & Illustration: Joanna Dee
Production Coordinator: Katie Beiter

Find us online at **www.avocado–highway.com**
Follow us on Instagram **@AvocadoHighway**

This book is dedicated to our friends, family, and avocado lovers around the globe. Get ready to hop on the avocado highway!

"WE ALL EAT, AND IT WOULD BE A SAD WASTE OF OPPORTUNITY TO EAT BADLY."
– ANNA THOMAS

CONTENTS

01
VEGAN

02
DAIRY

03
EGGS, FISH & MEAT

04
DESSERT

FOREWORD

Food Liberation, a health food store in New York City, has been in my family since 1976. It was initially run by my father, John Miklatek Sr., who imparted to me all the necessities of running a customer-centric business. Our store continues on with occasional reinventions, though never straying from the core mission of awakening people to the divine intention and power of natural food and medicine.

Avocados have myriad health benefits, are delicious and affordable. They are surely the most impressive of all fruits. Not only do they influence blood pressure and eye health, they also assist in keeping a proper cholesterol ratio. Though unusually high in fat for a fruit, their monounsaturated quality leads to cardiovascular protection, satiety, portion control and blood sugar balance. Pregnant or nursing women can ensure optimal folate levels by consuming them. Avocados also extend their properties to any condition characterized by inflammation due to their antioxidant and antiinflammatory rich nutrients. If this were not enough, consider that avocados increase the absorption of all fat soluble nutrients.

While this may be their first book, I don't think we have heard the last from Robi and Pamela. Each recipe is well planned, mouthwatering, and adheres to their styles of healthy living.

JOHN MIKLATEK *owner*
Food Liberation
1349 Lexington Avenue
New York City

INTRODUCTION

If you are reading this book, it's too late. Chances are, you are already an avocado lover like its founding team of women. We designed this book to be an easy way to take your avocado toast to the next level. The recipes are simple and easy, but in no way basic. They are divided by ingredient type to fit your dietary needs—we've got toasts for meat lovers, vegans, dairy queens, and those with a serious sweet tooth. Each recipe is paired with an artisanal bread, but don't be discouraged if you don't have that type; any bread will do. To continue on this theme of "versatility," these toasts are designed to be eaten any time of day—even when you're craving that midnight snack.

We want you to forage your pantry and use ingredients you have on hand. We have come to realize that pretty much anything with an avocado is tasty, even peanut butter cups. Think of this book as your "avocado bible"—but feel free to take the scripture loosely and create your own meaning.

Now, buckle up and join us for a ride on the Avocado Highway. It's sure to be an adventure.

xx,
ROBI & PAMELA

ABOUT THE AUTHORS

Robi Kellerman

As a health educator for over 20 years, Robi has devoted her life to promoting health and wellness. She received her Master's Degree in Public Health from New York University and completed her Health Coach certification through the Institute for Integrative Nutrition. In both her personal and professional spheres, she has always approached life from a holistic and health conscious standpoint, which has greatly enabled her clients to succeed.

Her many interests include health coaching, cooking, photography, flying airplanes, yoga, and volunteering at hospitals with her therapy dog, Mellow. With Avocado Highway, she has merged two of her passions—love of photography and cooking—in her first published cookbook.

Follow her Instagram @AvocadoHighway to stay up to date with new recipes and other avocado–themed ideas she has cooked up!

Pamela Fink

An innovator with a creative soul, Pamela Fink is known for her special requests at restaurants. She transforms ordinary dishes on the menu into something special with her substitutions and replacements, often adding avocado—a lifelong favorite food. Pamela's friends will be the first to say, "Let Pam do the ordering."

As owner and designer of Good Charma, Pamela is known for jewelry that inspires peace, harmony, love, and unity.

Her love of design, food, and health has led Pamela to co-create a book that takes her obsession of avocados to the next level, and allows her to share her avocado creations with others. For Pamela, life is a journey, a (avocado) highway filled with adventure, and she believes that all roads are open.

Follow her Instagram @AvocadoHighway and @GoodCharma to check out her spiritually motivated jewelry!

BUYING + OPENING AVOCADOS

How to Buy an Avocado

While there are several types of avocados, we use the Haas variety for our recipes. They constitute roughly 80% of the avocado market worldwide and are generally the easiest to find in grocery stores.

When shopping for an avocado, we like to perform the "squeeze test." Gently place the avocado in your palm and lightly squeeze it to determine its ripeness. A ripe, fresh avocado will not be hard nor will it be fully mushy—it will be somewhere in the middle. Once you buy your avocado, you have a day or two to eat it before it goes bad. If you want to buy an avocado that will last a little longer in your kitchen, make sure to buy one that is firmer.

How to Open an Avocado

After you've brought your perfect avocado home and you've decided it's time to make one of our toasts, you need to open it properly. We suggest slicing the avocado into two halves, removing the pit, and peeling the skin. Then, squeeze a little lemon juice to preserve the green color. When you're ready to eat, our recipes will guide you to dice, slice, smash, or scoop the avocado onto the toast for maximum tastiness. *Enjoy!*

INGREDIENTS IN YOUR KITCHEN

Breads

Bread has always brought people together—we at Avocado Highway love the idea of breaking bread with the ones we love—carbs don't count then. Bread is the vehicle for these recipes and we have chosen specific bread types, these are just suggestions. Slice them thin or thick and toast them until they're burnt or don't toast them at all. It's whatever you like!

- Baguette
- Brioche
- Challah
- Chocolate
- Ciabatta
- Country
- Focaccia
- Multi-Grain, Sourdough Pullman
- Olive
- Pain de Seigle
- Pullman
- Seeded
- Seeded Grain
- Semolina
- Sourdough
- Whole Wheat
- Whole Wheat Boule
- Whole Wheat Multi-Grain
- Whole Wheat Sesame
- 8-grain

Sauces

Our recipes feature a variety of sauces, which are all easy staples of any stocked pantry. We've provided a few easy recipes for some sauces like pesto if you fancy; however, store bought works just as well!

- Dijon Mustard
- Extra-Virgin Olive Oil
- Fish Sauce
- Harissa
- Honey
- Mayonnaise

- Peanut Butter
- Pesto (see pg. 20 for recipe)
- Pomegranate Molasses
- Salsa
- Sesame Oil
- Spicy Mayonnaise
- Tahini (see pg. 20 for recipe)
- Truffle Oil

Cheeses

Probably our favorite ingredient, next to avocados. Make sure to always buy raw when you can—your insides will thank you!

- Berkshire Blue
- Brie
- Feta
- Goat—Herbed or Plain
- Manchego
- Mexican Blend
- Muenster
- Ricotta
- Roquefort
- Parmesan

Pantry

If you don't have some of these items in your pantry, our cookbook gives you the opportunity to round out your kitchen.

- Bacon
- Black Beans
- Black Sesame Seeds
- Bread and Butter Pickles
- Brown Sugar
- Canned Tuna (in water)
- Capers
- Cayenne Pepper
- Dried Chili Flakes
- Chili Powder
- Coconut Flakes
- Corn Nuts
- Furikake
- Hemp Seeds
- Peanut Butter Cups
- Pepper
- Pickled Ginger
- Pink Peppercorns
- Poppy Seeds
- Salt—Coarse, Flaky, or Smoked
- Shaved Dark Chocolate
- Sesame Seeds
- Smoked Paprika
- Sunflower Seeds
- Walnuts

PANTRY RECIPES

Pesto

2 cups fresh basil leaves
¼ cup pine nuts
¼ cup walnut pieces
2 cloves garlic
¾ cup grated Parmesan cheese
2 teaspoons salt
1 cup pure olive oil

Put the basil, pine nuts, walnut pieces, garlic, Parmesan, and salt into a food processor and purée. With the machine running, slowly drizzle in the olive oil (you may not need the full amount) and process until the mixture resembles mayonnaise. The pesto can be made ahead and refrigerated for up to 4 days or frozen for 6 to 8 months; be sure to seal the top of the pesto with thin film of olive oil before covering.

Recipe courtesy of Susan Simon, "The Nantucket Table" (Chronicle Books, 1998)

Tahini

Juice of ½ lemon
1 teaspoon salt
2 tablespoons tahini paste
4 tablespoons warm water

In a small bowl, mix lemon juice, salt, and tahini paste. Whisk until combined. While mixing, add lukewarm water until desired consistency is reached.

Pan-Roasted Cherry Tomatoes

Add the olive oil to a medium skillet over medium heat. When the oil is warm, add cherry tomatoes and toss to thoroughly coat with the oil. Sauté, stirring occasionally until tomatoes are soft and blistered about 6–8 minutes.

Pan-Roasted Carrots

Add the olive oil to a medium skillet over medium heat. When the oil is warm add carrots, salt and pepper to taste, and toss to thoroughly coat with the oil. Sauté, stirring occasionally until the carrots are tender and slightly browned 8–10 minutes.

01

VEGAN

TRAINING WHEELS

The template for all toasts, the Training Wheels, steers you back to basics. But, easy rider, everything takes time to learn. Once you're done practicing in your kitchen, roll up your sleeves, rev up, and hit the highway with your own creations or try some of ours.

. . . .

INGREDIENTS

2 slices 8-grain bread, toasted

1 clove garlic, peeled, smashed

1 avocado, halved, pitted, mashed

1 tablespoon extra-virgin olive oil

1 pinch coarse or flaky sea salt

SERVES 2

DIRECTIONS

Rub the smashed garlic on the toast. Top with a generous layer of avocado. Garnish with a drizzle of extra-virgin olive oil and a sprinkle of sea salt.

THE ZINGER

Put a little zing in your avocado swing. Add lime zest. Simple but oh, so good!

. . . .

INGREDIENTS

2 slices country bread, toasted

1 avocado, halved, pitted, mashed

Grated zest of ½ lime

1 pinch smoked salt, or to taste

1 pinch cayenne pepper, or
to taste

SERVES 2

DIRECTIONS

Spread a luxurious amount of avocado mash on toast. Sprinkle with lime zest, salt, and cayenne.

BEJEWELED

This toast features pomegranates and figs, two of the Seven Species—a biblical food group native to Israel. The jewel of all fruits—the pomegranate is high in antioxidants, vitamin C, and vibrant in color. Its sensual counterpart, the fig, is full of fiber and potassium. Be a queen for the day and bejewel your toast regally.

. . . .

INGREDIENTS

2 slices focaccia, thinly sliced, toasted

1 avocado, halved, pitted, mashed

2 fresh figs, quartered

¼ cup pomegranate seeds

Coarse or flaky sea salt

Optional garnish: arugula leaves

SERVES 2

DIRECTIONS

Spread the avocado on toasted bread. Decorate with figs and pomegranate seeds. Top with a light sprinkle of sea salt. Garnish with arugula if desired.

MAGIC MAITAKE

You may not trip on the variety of fungi piled on this toast, but you will fall in love with it. Maitake mushrooms, also known as hen-of-the-woods, are used medicinally in Japan, and China. Here, we sauté them with garlic for a savory finish.

. . . .

INGREDIENTS

2 slices whole wheat sesame bread, toasted

½ package, Maitake mushrooms

1 tablespoon extra-virgin olive oil

1 clove garlic, finely chopped

1 avocado, halved, pitted, thinly sliced

1 pinch sea salt

2 teaspoons truffle oil

SERVES 2

DIRECTIONS

Add the extra-virgin olive oil to a medium skillet over medium heat. When the oil is warm, add the garlic and sauté until lightly browned, about 1–2 minutes. Add the mushrooms and sauté, stirring occasionally until the mushrooms are crisp and golden, about 5 minutes. Place the avocado on each slice of toast. Divide the mushrooms and add to the toasts. Sprinkle with salt, and drizzle the truffle oil over the top to serve.

ALT (AVOCADO, LETTUCE + TOMATO)

A vegan, modern twist on the American BLT classic, replacing bacon with avocado. You will still maintain the crunch of the sandwich by shredding romaine lettuce into narrow strips using a knife, or your fingers.

. . . .

INGREDIENTS

2 slices focaccia, toasted

1 avocado, halved, pitted, mashed

2 large romaine lettuce leaves, shredded

1 large tomato, thickly sliced

Coarse, flaky, or smoked sea salt

Freshly ground black pepper

1 tablespoon extra–virgin olive oil

SERVES 2

DIRECTIONS

Spread the avocado over each piece of focaccia. Lay shredded lettuce on top of the avocado. Top with tomato slices. Garnish with a sprinkle of sea salt, or smoked salt and freshly ground pepper. Drizzle with extra–virgin olive oil.

ELOTE

Elote, roasted corn, is a Mexican street food favorite. While our version doesn't feature Cotija cheese garnish, this tangy toast will bring out the inner spiciness in you.

. . . .

2 slices baguette cut on a broad diagonal, toasted

2 teaspoons extra-virgin olive oil

Kernels scraped from 1 ear corn

1 pinch salt, or to taste

1 avocado, halved, pitted, diced

¼ teaspoon dried chili flakes

Grated zest of ½ lime

SERVES 2

DIRECTIONS

Add the extra-virgin olive oil to a skillet over medium heat. When the oil is warm, about 1–2 minutes, add the corn kernels and salt. Toss to thoroughly coat with the oil. Sauté, stirring occasionally until the corn is golden—some kernels may even start to pop—about 7–10 minutes.

Spread the avocado on toast. Top with the pan-roasted corn. Sprinkle dried chili flakes and lime zest. Serve with a margarita or cerveza.

HOLY KALE

Maybe the healthiest toast in this book, the Holy Kale will have you backing that hass up and straight to the loo. We used a gluten free, seeded bread for this recipe. Monty Python never ate so healthy.

. . . .

INGREDIENTS

2 slices seeded bread, toasted

½ apple, your choice, halved, cored, julienned

1 teaspoon, fresh lemon juice

1 avocado, halved, pitted, sliced

2 kale leaves, shredded

¼ cup sunflower seeds, raw or lightly toasted

SERVES 2

DIRECTIONS

Toss the apple slices with lemon juice to prevent them from turning brown. Top toast with avocado slices. Divide the apple and pile on toasts. Top with shredded kale. Garnish with sunflower seeds.

THE GREEK GODHASS

Tahini, a much used ingredient in Middle Eastern kitchens, is a paste made from ground, hulled sesame seeds. Top on your local tomatoes and, with one bite, you'll feel like you're floating in the Dead Sea.

. . . .

INGREDIENTS

2 slices sourdough, toasted

1 avocado, halved, pitted, sliced

1 pint, fresh cherry tomatoes, roasted (*see pg. 19 for recipe*)

1 pinch sea salt

1 pinch fresh black pepper

2 tablespoons tahini
(*see pg. 18 for recipe*)

1 pinch toasted or black sesame seeds

Juice of ½ lemon

1 sprig of thyme, leaves removed

SERVES 2

DIRECTIONS

Place avocado slices on toast. Cover with roasted cherry tomatoes. Drizzle with tahini sauce. Garnish with a pinch of toasted or black sesame seeds and lemon juice, if desired. Top with fresh thyme.

SWEET BEANS

A veggie patty on toast, you'll want this one the most.
Sweet Beans is good for your heart, top with lime to make it tart.
A sweet potato will add some pop, put it on the bottom or layer on top!

. . . .

2 slices sourdough, toasted

1 avocado, halved, pitted, cut into
2-inch chunks

Juice of ½ lime

1 pinch ground chili powder

1 tablespoon chopped fresh
cilantro

1/2 mashed, baked, peeled
sweet potato

1/2 can black beans

1 pinch sesame seeds

DIRECTIONS

In a small bowl add the avocado
with lime juice, chili powder and
half of the chopped cilantro.
Spread on toast. Top with mashed
sweet potatoes and black beans.
Garnish with remaining chopped
cilantro and sesame seeds.

SERVES 2

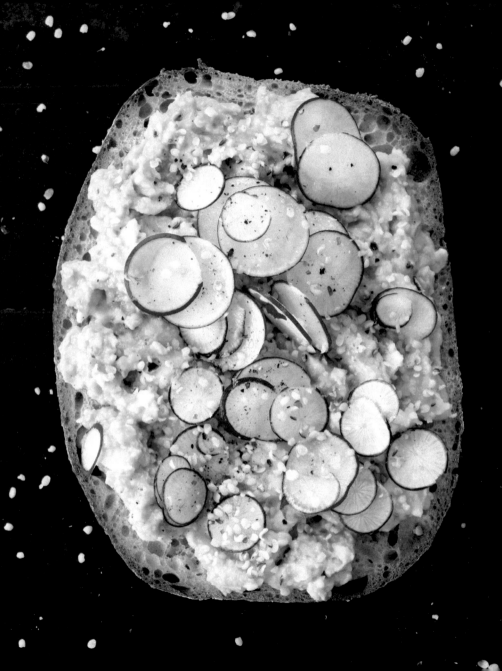

AVOCADO HIGHWAY

You won't get high, but you will get healthy eating our namesake. Hemp seeds, which taste like soft sunflower seeds, aid with digestion, weight loss, and are high in protein. They are a nutritionist's dream! Sliced radishes add a crunchy finish.

. . . .

INGREDIENTS

2 slices focaccia, toasted

1 avocado, halved, pitted, mashed

4 medium radishes, thinly sliced

1 tablespoon hemp seeds

Extra–virgin olive oil

Coarse or flaky sea salt

Freshly ground black pepper

SERVES 2

DIRECTIONS

Spread avocado on each piece of toast. Generously top with sliced radishes. Sprinkle with hemp seeds. Garnish with a drizzle of extra–virgin olive oil and a pinch of salt and pepper.

02

DAIRY

ROCK THE GOAT

Vote for the goat, no cow for now. We want YOU to top with cherry tomatoes and olive oil for a savory finish. No elephants or donkeys please.

. . . .

INGREDIENTS

2 slices sourdough, toasted

1 avocado, halved, pitted, thinly sliced

Handful cherry tomatoes, halved

2 ounces plain or herbed goat cheese at room temperature

1 tablespoon extra-virgin olive oil

Coarse or flaky sea salt

Freshly ground black pepper

SERVES 2

DIRECTIONS

Place the avocado on each slice of toast. Cover avocado with tomato slices. With a spoon, dollop goat cheese on top of tomatoes. Drizzle with extra-virgin olive oil. Garnish with salt and freshly ground pepper.

MERCI, BRIE CUKE

Who needs fondue when you can have the Versailles of all toasts? A baguette, a bicycle, and a wheel of brie are all you need to feel like a Frenchie for a day. Merci Beaucoup and bon appetit!

. . . .

INGREDIENTS

2 slices Pain de Seigle, toasted

1 avocado, halved, pitted, mashed

3–4 ounces Brie at room temperature, cut into wedges

1 cucumber, sliced

Fresh herbs, such as chervil, tarragon, or dill

SERVES 2

DIRECTIONS

Spread the avocado on toasted bread. Top with Brie wedges and cucumber slices. Garnish with fresh herbs. Glass of Rosé, optional.

ITALIAN STALLION

This is one sexy toast. With a little slice of pesto heaven, featuring the color of the Italian flag, you can pretend you're on a Roman Holiday enjoying *la dolce vita*. Gregory Peck not included.

. . . .

INGREDIENTS

2 slices Ciabatta, toasted

1 avocado, halved, pitted

1 large tomato, diced

2 tablespoons, pesto
(*see pg. 20 for recipe*)

1 teaspoon extra-virgin olive oil

1 pinch coarse or flaky sea salt

1 pinch freshly ground black pepper

Handful fresh basil leaves

1 tablespoon grated Parmesan cheese

SERVES 2

DIRECTIONS

Place half avocado on each piece of toast. Top with diced tomatoes and large droplets of pesto. Drizzle with extra-virgin olive oil, salt, pepper, basil leaves, and a shower of Parmesan.

NANF*CKIT

There once was a man from Nantucket
Who carried 'cados in his bucket.
He said with a grin while sipping his gin,
I'm eating my toast so Nanf*ckit!

. . . .

INGREDIENTS

2 slices sourdough, toasted

¼ cup whole milk ricotta cheese

1 avocado, halved, pitted

1 teaspoon pink peppercorns

4 large fresh basil leaves, shredded

SERVES 2

DIRECTIONS

Spoon the ricotta onto the toast.
Use a melon baller to scoop
bite–sized rounds of avocado
onto the cheese. Crumble pink
peppercorns over the toast.
Garnish with fresh basil.

THE MUENSTER MASH

Perfect for all you Zombies who need an easy toast to assemble. Use as much mustard as you please and don't forget to melt the muenster cheese.

. . . .

INGREDIENTS

2 slices whole wheat Pullman, toasted

1 tablespoon mustard, such as whole grain Dijon

1 avocado, halved, pitted, mashed

2 slices Muenster cheese

Bread and butter pickles

SERVES 2

DIRECTIONS

Spread mustard on toasted bread and top with mashed avocado. Cover with cheese and bake until edges have browned. Garnish with bread and butter pickles

THE BOSWELL

"Take something you know you love and put it on avocado toast and you will be happier," our food stylist, Frances Boswell, said to us one day. Similar to working with her, this recipe is smooth, easy, and simple. And, it will leave you feeling happy and healthy.

. . . .

INGREDIENTS

2 slices semolina bread, toasted

1 avocado, halved, pitted, mashed

2 ounces chevre, room temperature

2 large roasted carrots, sliced into quarters (*see pg. 21 for recipe*)

1 pinch coarse or flaky sea salt, or to taste

2 tablespoons toasted sunflower seeds

1 tablespoon extra-virgin olive oil

SERVES 2

DIRECTIONS

Spread the avocado on the toast. Generously layer chevre on top. Cover with roasted carrots. Garnish with toasted sunflower seeds and a splash of extra-virgin olive oil.

FIESTA FOREVER

Fiesta, forever, allllll night long! With salsa, cheese, onions, and hot peppers, this "Mexcellent" toast is one big party featuring everything but the kitchen sink.

. . . .

2 slices olive bread, toasted

1 avocado, halved, pitted, sliced

2 tablespoons salsa

2 tablespoons finely chopped red onion

1 teaspoon hot pepper such as jalapeño, Thai, or cayenne, minced

¼ cup Mexican cheese, such as queso blanco or a shredded Mexican cheese blend

2 tablespoons corn nuts

1 tablespoon, chopped fresh cilantro

SERVES 2

Place avocado slices on toast. Top avocado with salsa, red onion, and hot peppers. Sprinkle cheese on top. Garnish with corn nuts and fresh cilantro. Serve immediately con una cerveza.

TREND FETA

Microgreens are salad shoots that have been picked just after the first leaves have developed. The mayo and feta accessorize this otherwise spare toast with a little bit of style.

. . . .

2 slices whole wheat multi–grain, toasted

2 tablespoons spicy mayonnaise

1 avocado, halved, pitted, sliced

¼ cup feta cheese, crumbled

1 handful micro greens or pea shoots

Freshly ground black pepper

SERVES 2

DIRECTIONS

Spread a layer of spicy mayonnaise on each piece of toast. Place the avocado slices on top. Cover with the feta. Top with a handful of micro greens or pea shoots. Garnish with a grind of fresh black pepper.

BETTAH WITH FETA

What's pink, white, and green all over? No, not that bikini you've been eyeing. It's the Bettah with Feta! Featuring thin slices of fresh watermelon, this toast is sure to cool you off on a hot summer day.

INGREDIENTS

2 slices olive bread, toasted

1 avocado, halved, pitted, sliced

Small wedge watermelon, thinly sliced

2 ounces feta cheese, crumbled or sliced

1 teaspoon poppy seeds

SERVES 2

DIRECTIONS

Place avocado slices on toast. Top with sliced watermelon and feta cheese. Garnish with a pinch of poppy seeds.

AUTUMN IN THE BERKSHIRES

Might we suggest a ride up Route 7 from Great Barrington to Stockbridge, Massachusetts on a cool Autumn day? Stop by your local farm stand and pick up some Berkshire Blue and then find your favorite fireplace and cozy up with the cheesiest of toasts.

. . . .

INGREDIENTS

2 slices whole wheat boule, toasted

5 ounces Berkshire Blue Cheese, or Roquefort

1 avocado, halved, pitted, sliced

1 hard–ish pear, such as Bosc or Anjou, cored, quartered

¼ cup walnuts chopped, toasted

SERVES 2

DIRECTIONS

Spread toast with a rich, generous layer of softened blue cheese. Cover with avocado slices. Top with pears. Garnish with chopped walnuts.

03

EGGS, FISH, & MEAT

EVIL EYE

Ward off all of your Xs, Ys, and Zs with this avocado toast. Guaranteed to protect you, this fried egg is no yoke!

. . . .

INGREDIENTS

2 slices Ciabatta, trimmed, toasted

1 avocado, halved, pitted, mashed

1 tablespoon butter or extra-virgin olive oil

2 fresh eggs

Coarse or flaky sea salt

Freshly ground black pepper

Optional garnish: fresh or dried chili flakes, or Harissa

SERVES 2

DIRECTIONS

Spread the avocado onto each slice of toast. Heat butter or oil in small skillet over medium-high heat until the butter has melted or the oil is warm. Break the eggs and carefully slip them into skillet and fry until whites are golden brown around the edges, and the yolk is set, about 2–3 minutes. Transfer to top of the toast. Sprinkle salt, freshly ground black pepper, and the optional chili, or harissa, over the top. Serve immediately.

SIMON SAYS

Our friend, Susan Simon says, "I use slices of toasted, multi-grain sourdough Pullman loaf because the square shape can be cut on the diagonal, keeping half an egg on each piece—that way the first bite comes from a pointed corner. The garnish of a drizzle of dense, sticky, pomegranate molasses, combined with a sprinkle of salty, crunchy Furikake - the Japanese mixture of black sesame seeds and bonito flakes - makes for a perfect combination of flavor and texture."

. . . .

INGREDIENTS

2 slices multi–grain sourdough Pullman, toasted

2 tablespoons extra–virgin olive oil

2 eggs, hard–cooked (approx. 8 minutes)

1 avocado, halved, pitted, chopped

1 ½ teaspoons pomegranate molasses

1 ½ teaspoons Furikake

SERVES 2

DIRECTIONS

Place each toast on a plate. Drench each slice with a tablespoon of extra–virgin olive oil. Spread the avocado over each toast. Cut the eggs in half, place the two halves on each toast. Drizzle the pomegranate molasses over each toast. Sprinkle with the Furikake. Cut in half on the diagonal.

SEAS THE MOMENT

Packed with protein, this Asian-inspired dish will leave you full and energized for hours. Top with lime juice and sesame oil for a toast that is not your everyday "Chicken of the Sea."

. . . .

INGREDIENTS

2 slices whole wheat Pullman, toasted

2 teaspoons sesame oil

4 ounces sushi grade Ahi Tuna loin

1 avocado, halved, pitted, sliced

1 tablespoon pickled ginger

1 pinch black sesame seeds

SERVES 2

DIRECTIONS

Drizzle sesame oil into a skillet. On medium-high heat, place tuna loin in skillet. Cook on all sides until seared, about 5 minutes.

Place avocado slices on toast. Top with seared, sliced ahi tuna. Place pickled ginger, sesame seeds, and a drizzle of sesame oil on the tuna.

LOX NESS

The Loch Ness Monster, also known as Nessie, is a mythical creature that lives in Loch Ness in the Scottish Highlands. Swimming around her is some of our favorite salmon. Top it on your avocado toast for a smokin' good lunch.

. . . .

INGREDIENTS

2 slices sourdough, toasted

1 avocado, halved, pitted, sliced

4–6 slices extra thin Nova or Smoked Salmon

¼ small cucumber, julienned

1 large radish, julienned

¼ small red onion, thinly sliced

1 heaping teaspoon capers

1 pinch chopped fresh dill

SERVES 2

DIRECTIONS

Place avocado slices on top of toasted sourdough. Drape the Nova or smoked salmon over the avocado. Top with cucumber and radishes. Garnish with capers and a shower of dill.

There are two different types of Smoked Salmon—nordic and Scottish. Nordic Smoked Salmon is salt cured and cold smoked, Scottish Smoked Salmon is dry-brined and cold smoked. We recommend the Scottish version here.

BANH MI–CADO

This toast will definitely bring you some good karma. Take your classic tuna on an Asian adventure with this DIY Banh Mi. The lemongrass, cilantro, and ginger will spice up your Zen.

. . . .

INGREDIENTS

½ classic baguette, sliced in half horizontally, toasted

1 can or jar of solid white tuna in water

1 inch lemongrass, finely chopped

1 quarter red onion, chopped, plus a few thin slices for garnish

1 inch ginger, peeled and chopped

2 tablespoons fresh lemon juice

1 teaspoon fish sauce (optional)

1 teaspoon extra–virgin olive oil

1 pinch dried chili flakes

Small handful fresh cilantro, chopped

1 avocado, halved, peeled, sliced

SERVES 2

DIRECTIONS

Drain tuna and put in a bowl. Add the chopped lemongrass, red onion, ginger to the tuna and combine. Add lemon juice, fish sauce (if using), and some olive oil to moisten. Sprinkle with dried chili flakes and ½ chopped fresh cilantro. Stir.

Assemble avocado slices on toasted bread. Top with tuna mixture and garnish with thinly sliced red onion and remaining fresh cilantro.

TAPAS ON TOAST

Tap into your toast and take a wild ride down the Spanish coast. Manchego is a Spanish cheese made from sheep's milk. Firm with a buttery taste, it's super versatile and melts well, too! Spanish Chorizo is a dried, cured smoked pork sausage. It can be sliced and eaten as is, casings and all, and this is what we use here.

INGREDIENTS

2 slices Ciabatta, thinly sliced

1 avocado, halved, pitted, sliced

8 thin slices Chorizo

8 thin slices Manchego

Smoked paprika for garnish

SERVES 2

DIRECTIONS

Toast the thinly sliced Ciabatta until crostini–like. Place avocado slices on top. Top with chorizo and manchego. Garnish with a dusting of smoked paprika.

THE BACONTARIAN CLUB

A favourite of King Edward VIII of England and his American wife, Wallis Simpson, we substitute avocado for chicken in our version of the club sandwich. Thick slices of bacon, lettuce, tomato, and onion are cradled in between two pieces of white Pullman slathered in organic mayonnaise.

. . . .

INGREDIENTS

2 slices white Pullman, toasted

4 strips applewood smoked bacon

2 tablespoons, mayonnaise

1 avocado, halved, pitted, sliced

1 large tomato, sliced

½ yellow onion, thinly sliced

1 pinch sea salt

1 pinch freshly ground pepper

SERVES 2

DIRECTIONS

Place four strips of bacon in a skillet over medium–high heat. Cook until crisp. Spread a layer of mayonnaise on toast. Place avocado slices on top. Cover with tomato and onion slices. Top with bacon strips. Garnish with salt and pepper as needed. Feel free to stack up the slices for that old school club look.

04

DESSERT

PB&A

Hey! You put your peanut butter in my avocado! Hey! You put your avocado in my peanut butter! No, this isn't your classic peanut butter cup. Our version is for all you baby boomers out there still rocking the highway-sted look.

. . . .

INGREDIENTS

2 slices chocolate bread, toasted

4 tablespoons organic peanut butter

1 avocado, halved, pitted, sliced

1 pinch sea salt

Shaved dark chocolate, or Justin's dark chocolate peanut butter cups, chopped

SERVES 2

DIRECTIONS

Generously spread peanut butter on toast. Top with sliced avocados. Cover with shaved chocolate, or dark chocolate peanut butter cups. Garnish with a sprinkle of sea salt. Serve with a glass of cold milk and some wet wipes—you will need them.

83

BANANA SPLIT

A little banana, some shredded coconut, and a drizzle of honey are the tools you need to weather the storm, whatever it may be. This sweet treat can be eaten 24/7.

. . . .

INGREDIENTS

2 slices challah or
Brioche bread, toasted

2 teaspoons shredded
unsweetened coconut

1 avocado, halved, pitted, chopped

1 banana, sliced

2 tablespoons liquid honey

½ teaspoon flaky sea salt

SERVES 2

DIRECTIONS

Lightly toast the shredded coconut in a dry skillet, tossing constantly—to prevent it from burning—until light brown, just under a minute.

Place avocado slices on toasted bread. (If you are using challah, keep an eye on the slices as they toast easily.) Arrange the banana slices on the avocado. Sprinkle a handful of coconut over the toast and garnish with a drizzle of honey and flaky sea salt.

BEA'S BRAZILIAN BREAKFAST

Our Brazilian photographer, Bea, has been eating this avocado toast since she was a little girl. A splash of lime and a pinch of brown sugar will have you daydreaming about parading around Rio de Janiero in a teeny, tiny bikini.

INGREDIENTS

2 slices seeded grain, toasted

1 avocado, halved, pitted, sliced

1 lime, halved

1 tablespoon brown sugar

SERVES 2

DIRECTIONS

Squeeze lime onto each avocado half. Drizzle with brown sugar. With a spoon, scoop avocado out and eat with a side of toasted bread.

CONVERSION CHARTS

CUP	TBSP	TSP	ML
1 cup	16 Tbsp	48 tsp	240 ml
¾ cup	12 Tbsp	36 tsp	180 ml
⅔ cup	11 Tbsp	32 tsp	160 ml
½ cup	8 Tbsp	24 tsp	120 ml
⅓ cup	5 Tbsp	16 tsp	80 ml
¼ cup	4 Tbsp	12 tsp	60 ml
—	1 Tbsp	—	15 ml
—	—	1 tsp	5 ml

US TO METRIC CONVERSIONS	
⅕ tsp	1 ml
1 tsp	5 ml
1 Tbsp	15 ml
1 oz	30 ml
1/5 cup	50 ml
1 cup	240 ml
2 cups (1 pint)	470 ml

CUP	OUNCES
1 cup	8 fl oz
¾ cup	6 fl oz
⅔ cup	5 fl oz
½ cup	4 fl oz
⅓ cup	3 fl oz
¼ cup	2 fl oz

ACKNOWLEDGMENTS

This book would not have been possible without the love and support of several people. Thank you Steven Meltzer aka Papa Bear for overnighting avocados for our photo shoot. Thank you Robin Walther, Sheilaa Hite, Amy Roth, Dulci Carroll, and Barbara Riering for all of your encouragement and guidance. And, a BIG thank you to Katie Beiter, our production coordinator, editor, and social media expert—you were our anchor throughout this entire process.

Thanks, especially, to the Avocado man for donating two whole cases of Hass avocados for our photo shoots; Berkshire Mountain Bakery for supplying all of our fabulous artisanal breads; Indian Line Farm for constantly providing fresh farm to fork produce; and, lastly a huge thank you to our all-time favorite grocery store, Guido's, for always having everything we need, even Furikake.